Endorsements

"Olga is inviting you to go to a fun school she affectionately calls Happiness School. I love this book and the joy it brings to the world. Happiness is something within everyone's reach. Choose to devour every word of this great book and begin to experience happiness unlike anything you have ever experienced before."

—Peggy McColl,
New York Times Best-Selling Author
http://PeggyMcColl.com

Happiness by You by Olga Dewar is a refreshing, upliftinging read full of joy and positivity. A beautiful guide, this book will enable you to look within yourself to find happiness in the most mundane situations, helping you to realize that happiness is a state of mind and not the result of your circumstances.

—Judy O'Beirn,
President & CEO of Hasmark Publishing International

"I love how the book begins! I was taken off guard but got a pleasurable and happy feeling at first sight. I am connecting to the author at once, and especially to the subject. It is 'right up my face' in a refreshing way, and I like it. I get to go on a journey that this wonderful author has made, and she lets me inside in an open and welcoming way. And to top it all off, she has created exercises for me! This book is very personal and beautifully written. It will make many people start thinking about whether they are really doing something about their own situation. Happiness is a CHOICE, and if you do not understand what I mean by that, then you need to read the book. Well, you should read it anyway!"

—Ki is your host,
author of *WALK TALL –*
Create Your Own Self-Confidence (the guide book)

Is there a formula for happiness? Maybe not but Olga Dewar has it down to a science. Encouraging readers to focus greatly on their personal mindset, Olga has a unique approach to the pursuit of happiness. Truly believing that happiness is a choice, she takes her readers on a magical journey full of guidelines and exercises to Happiness School. This was a wonderful and uplifting read and I highly recommend it for readers of all ages!

—Kathleen Cameron,
Author of Becoming the One

HAPPINESS BY YOU

By
Olga Dewar

Hasmark
PUBLISHING
INTERNATIONAL

Published by Hasmark Publishing
www.hasmarkpublishing.com

Copyright © 2021 Olga Dewar

First Edition

No part of this book may be reproduced or transmitted in any form or by any means, electronic or mechanical, including photocopying, recording or by any information storage and retrieval system, without written permission from the author, except for the inclusion of brief quotations in a review.

Disclaimer

This book is designed to provide information and motivation to our readers. It is sold with the understanding that the publisher is not engaged to render any type of psychological, legal, or any other kind of professional advice. The content of each article is the sole expression and opinion of its author, and not necessarily that of the publisher. No warranties or guarantees are expressed or implied by the publisher's choice to include any of the content in this volume. Neither the publisher nor the individual author(s) shall be liable for any physical, psychological, emotional, financial, or commercial damages, including, but not limited to, special, incidental, consequential or other damages. Our views and rights are the same: You are responsible for your own choices, actions, and results.

Permission should be addressed in writing to Olga at olga@happinessbyyou.com

Editor: Judith Scott judith@hasmarkpublishing.com
Cover Designer: Olga Dewar olga@happinessbyyou.com
Book Designer: Amit Dey amit@hasmarkpublishing.com

ISBN 13: 978-1-77482-030-8
ISBN 10: 1774820307

Dedicated to the strong women in my family:
Mom, Babushka, and Aunt Lena.
Thank you for being you and teaching me to be Me!

Table of Contents

Introduction ix
CHAPTER 1: The Definition of Happiness is a Definition of You. 1
CHAPTER 2: Things That Make You Happy 10
CHAPTER 3: Things That Interfere with Your Happiness 23
CHAPTER 4: Understanding Yourself 30
CHAPTER 5: Making Choices 41
CHAPTER 6: Happy at Last!. 50
About the Author. 55

Introduction

Hi! How are you? Are you doing well today? How about yesterday? Did you have a good day?

Whatever your answers are, I have just one more very simple question for you: Are you happy?

Please don't think about it too much. Just answer how you feel right now. So, why do you think you feel this way? Okay, maybe it is too early to ask.

Where do we start?

How about with the following question: Do you consider yourself a happy person?

I know it is difficult to be happy every day. So, how often are you happy? Every day? A few times a week? A few times a month? A few times a year?

Have you ever thought about what makes you happy? And, if you are not happy as often as you'd like to be, have you ever thought why?

Okay, okay, I know, too many questions right from the get go. So, let's ease into it and see what's with all of the questions.

I believe I have now mastered the feeling of happiness, and I would love to share my knowledge with you.

Gratitude is an everyday action in my world, and as I am starting to write this book on Thanksgiving Sunday of 2016, I cannot help but feel grateful for my life and everything in it. And even though right now my life is full of things that could send one into a deep depression, I am very happy!

I am happy to be alive, happy to be healthy, happy to be me!

Thank you, Universe, for all that I have! My life is better than I could ever imagine!

So, whatever your answers to the above questions were, I hope this book can help you to feel happy more often. And even if you are happy all of the time, I greatly appreciate you giving this book your time.

This book is like a textbook (yes, I am asking you to go back to school – Happiness School), and each chapter is a lesson. And of course, no lesson is without a little homework (#sorrynotsorry).

You will find the assignments in a separate workbook. It is very important for you to complete the assignment before moving to the next chapter.

To access your complimentary workbook, please visit HAPPINESSBYYOU.COM and join the HBY community.

Without further delay, let's have a look at the concept of happiness in more detail.

Welcome to the happiness journey!

CHAPTER 1

The Definition of Happiness is a Definition of You

How do you start a book about happiness? I suppose there are a few options: with a happy story, happy memory, funny photo or happy inspirational phrase. However, I will forgo all of the above and start with the definition.

Yes, I believe it is important to understand the definition of the actual word **happiness** before we go any further. We will have a look at a few online suggestions:

1. Merriam-Webster's Dictionary:
   – A state of well-being and contentment, a pleasurable or satisfying experience.
2. Vocabulary.com:
   – Is that feeling that comes over you when you know life is good and you can't help but smile. A sense of well-being, joy, or contentment.

3. Dictionary.com
   – The quality or state of being happy; good fortune; pleasure; contentment; joy.

It seems that now you should have a better understanding of the meaning of the word ***happiness***. According to the trusted online sources we should be happy when we are satisfied with our lives. That's it, very simple! I guess there is nothing else I can write about.

But not so fast! If you know me and follow my HBY Facebook page and Instagram posts, you know there is more to come. I always have an opinion and am happy (there is that word again) to share it with you.

So, now let's have a look at what makes you happy. Is it your family? Is it your work? Your favorite food or drink? Being on vacation? Travel? Holidays? Presents? Money? New clothes? New or favorite car? Seeing a favorite movie or reading a favorite book?

Let's face it, this list can be pretty long. I am sure I would not be able to cover all the things that can make a person happy.

I also think that at times happiness could be the combination of things – the right combination, if you know what I mean – just the right combination for you, a perfect match of circumstances!

But let's get back to the common suggestion in all three definitions of ***happiness*** we used – being content.

According to the definition there is nothing more for you to desire. You are happy with what you have, and that's the end of it.

I certainly agree that being happy with what you have is a great approach but if you are not desiring more, then there is nothing to strive for any longer. It can get quite boring and depressing not to have something new to achieve, well at least in my world. When one goal is reached, the next one is in line to be worked on. You are most likely on board with my thoughts and always desire something more.

Does this mean that we are unhappy if we desire more?

Of course not! Remember, it is practically impossible to be happy all of the time. It would be wonderful to feel elated constantly, but we are human beings with a wide range of emotions. And we expect very much to feel all of them – feeling happy is just one part of our life experience.

We feel sadness, worry, anger, frustration, indifference, love, jealousy, disgust, fear and many more emotions. Yes, some are not as pleasant as feeling happy, but all are part of life and without them I believe we are incomplete. And though they all deserve attention, in this book we will focus on the feeling of ***happiness***.

I suspect you are a little confused right now, and that is okay. As you read further, each page will bring more clarity.

So, let's think about happy people. We have all come across a few in our lifetime. These are the people who smile most of the time, and their smile is very infectious. They have a positive outlook on life no matter the circumstances. They are always friendly and happy to help a perfect stranger. And yes, these are the people who might be annoying to you if you are not a morning person. They are full of energy, spunky, and chatty even before you had your first coffee. They are simply high on life! Do you know the type?

Well, I am one of these people. And it is fun to be this way! It does not matter if it rains or shines; it does not matter if it's hot or cold; it does not matter if it's day or night. I am just happy! And it is difficult to dampen my state of mind on any given day. It feels great!

Here is what I'd like you to do next. Think about happy people in your world: family members, friends, or colleagues. Have you ever asked them why they are happy? If not, do so.

Maybe they never even thought about the reason; they just are happy. However, usually this question makes people think.

Happiness is a great feeling, and I am sure more people would like to have it more often. That is why it is imperative to understand what makes **YOU** happy. But we will discuss this in more detail (spoiler alert) in the next chapter. For now, we will return to understanding the definition of ***happiness***.

Have you ever thought about what defines you in life? Is it your family? Is it your job? Is it your past? Is it your present circumstances? Let me elaborate.

You probably figured out by now that I like people and have no issues talking to anyone, including striking up a conversation with a complete stranger. And at times some of these people have a tendency to open up to me and tell me their life stories just within a few minutes of our meeting.

I come across these people on a regular basis. I meet people from different walks of life, and no matter what social status, country of origin, religion, sexual orientation, or age they are, there seems to be a common theme among most of them – they complain about something. It might be their job, their health, their relationship, or their family. And when I happen to see one of these people on more than one occasion, the theme is the same.

Well, if we refer to the earlier definition of happiness, it will appear that these people are not content. They are unhappy with certain aspects of their lives. This is totally normal for all of us, even the happiest of us. The question is how do these individuals handle the situation? Are they doing anything to improve this area of their lives? Are they doing anything at all?

Unfortunately, in most cases I hear people complain about the same aspect over and over again. To be honest, I cannot stand it! It irritates me! And it has nothing to do with the person as an individual but the fact that nothing is being done. Do you understand me?

Let's have a look at an example. I am sure we all know someone (maybe it's you) who does not like their job. So, every time you meet this person all you hear is how much they dislike their job and wish that there was something better.

Okay, I accept the fact that you don't like it, so what are you doing about finding something that you enjoy more? Then I get: "It's great pay;" "I need this job;" "It has great benefits;" "I am a few years away from retirement," etc. After I hear any of the above, I usually suggest that perhaps it is not so bad. And then I get: "Yes, but …" At this point I will politely ask again: "So, what are you doing about it?"

Unfortunately, this usually shocks people. They are not prepared for such a reality check. They also rarely realize that constant dissatisfaction in one area of their lives can slowly seep through into other areas, thus affecting life in general. And then we can have a chain reaction: we get unhappy; our colleagues get unhappy dealing with us; our relationships get affected in a negative way; our families get affected; we have a fight with neighbours; our neighbourhood gets angry; the anger gets spilled on the street of the city, and the next thing you know, we have a war on our hands.

A little too dramatic for you? Well, what is a good book without drama!

But in all seriousness, this happens on a daily basis. So, I don't like people blaming circumstance on their discontent or lack of happiness.

I believe we are all in charge of our own happiness. If you are unhappy, there is work to be done. And we will get there in more detail in time.

Although, as a happy, compassionate person I struggle with this type of behaviour, I will try to listen and see if there is some way that I can help. As I mentioned earlier, I will ask a few questions and see if this will trigger something in the person. If it doesn't, I will offer my view of the circumstance and try to point out the positive aspects. It doesn't always work but it is worth trying.

Even if the individual disagrees with me and continues with their negative way, this person at least had a glimpse of how to turn the negative situation into a more positive one. And, perhaps every time this matter comes up in another conversation, it will trigger a memory of our discussion and bring positive thoughts. A person like me can hope!

In conclusion of this chapter, I encourage you to be wary of what defines you. We all go through positive and negative situations in our lives. That's just life. The important part to remember is to choose what will define you. Will it be a positive or negative situation in your life?

In order to help you figure this out, a key takeaway of this chapter is to have an awareness of what defines you. So, we will conclude our class (remember I mentioned school?) with an Assignment. There are no marks since I work with an honour system. This assignment should help you to find what defines ***your happiness***. Are you ready? Have you got your Assignment book yet? If not, go get it now at HAPPINESSBYYOU.COM and head to Assignment 1. We will reconnect in Chapter 2.

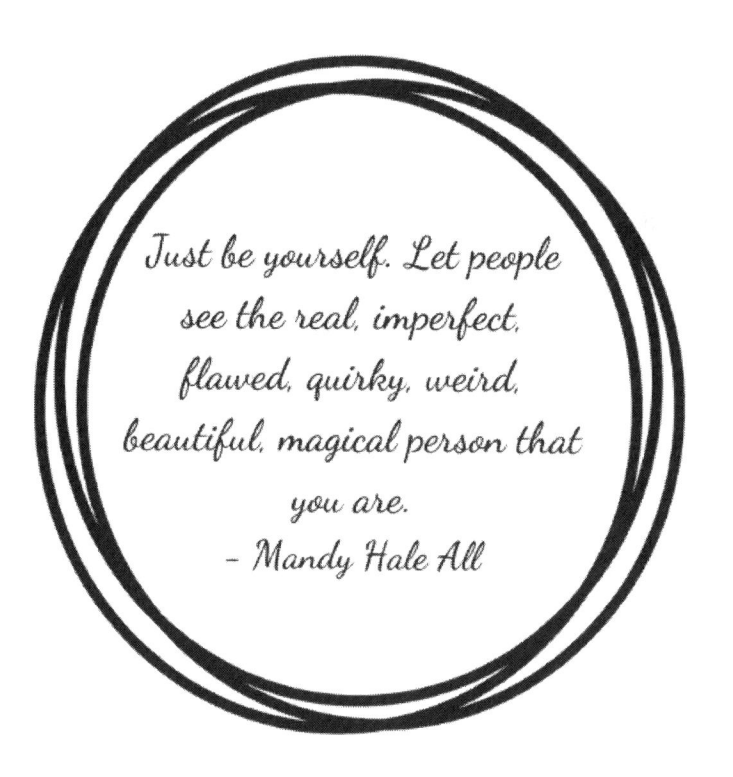

> Just be yourself. Let people see the real, imperfect, flawed, quirky, weird, beautiful, magical person that you are.
> – Mandy Hale All

CHAPTER 2

Things That Make You Happy

Oh, this will be such a fun chapter! What can be better than thinking of and remembering all of the things that make us happy? Just the thought of this puts a smile on my face! How about you?

As humans, we have common triggers that can make us happy. Here is just a short list:

- Food when you're hungry
- A warm blanket when you're cold
- A funny story
- A compliment directed at you
- Anticipation of something that excites you
- The completion of something that you've been working hard on for a while
- The arrival of a new baby
- The feeling of being in love

Are you with me on this? Well, I am sure you are, even if just for the first two items on the list. After all, we are all different and do not subscribe to the same way of life.

Now, let's have a look at some of the items above in more detail. Food and shelter are the basic needs of any individual. These are the first two aspects of survival for people. When we are hungry, we look for food; and when we are cold, we look for clothes or shelter to keep warm.

But we have evolved as humans and, eventually, raw meat and caves were no longer adequate to make us content. (Remember Chapter 1?) As time went on, the food needed to be cooked and the caves required windows and doors. From then on, things got even more developed: food developed flavour and caves evolved into dwellings with intricate designs detached from the mountains. As evolution progressed, humanity developed choices. And these days it is difficult to find an individual who would be satisfied with raw food and a bare-walled stone dwelling.

I can tell you that this is a pretty amazing phenomenon. As we grow, we are faced with this progression and making choices. And it seems that every day there are more and more choices to make. That alone is a reason for a smile!

But let's slow down a little and have a closer look at happy things in life. I will lead the way since I know myself the best.

Here are a few things or actions that make me happy:

- Sun
- Blue sky
- Nature in all its glory (yes, people, even the cold days)
- People I love
- Spirituality
- Feeling happy (I know, this sounds strange)
- Being active
- Singing
- Dancing

I did not take time to think about this list. I simply asked myself: "What makes me really happy?" And just like that, these were the first things that popped in my head as I wrote this part of the book.

Of course, these are not the only things that make me happy, but it seems they are the most important ones since it did not take any effort for them to reveal themselves. I just started typing without giving it much thought. And as I look at the list now, I would agree 100% that these are the top-rated happiness triggers in my life.

You might find it interesting that this "hit list" does not include anything material. There is no dream home, or fancy car, or high-end clothing, and precious jewels. I assure you that these are not foreign concepts to me. I am a human being after all. And I do not shy away from nice things that money can buy and happen to have a few.

But over the years of chasing the dream life I realized that material items did not make me happy in the long run. Actually, there was more negative energy around these possessions. It took a long time and deep understanding of self to realize that material things will not provide you with a constant feeling of elation (well, almost constant).

Please understand that I am not bashing the material world. I love money and would love to have more at any given time. I do not believe money is evil; I believe that people make money look bad. It is very sad to see when money is used to destroy lives, create wars to make more money, and intimidate people in a less fortunate position.

In my world money is used to better my life and my loved one's lives, to help a friend or a less fortunate person, to enrich nature, and to enhance the lives of others. When you give, you'll receive a lot more. One of my favorite things to do is to give gifts. And not just any gift. I try to put a lot of thought and heart into it. Just seeing the smile on the person's face when they open the wrapper gives me a high! Yes, this very simple act makes me very happy!

It took me a long time to get where I am today. And it has not been an easy road, but the experiences that I have encountered created this amazing life that I have now. I do not own a fancy home or drive a fancy car (as a matter of fact I do not own a home at all), my current income keeps me wondering if I can cover my monthly bills, and I am just wrapping up a part of my life that has been dragging me down for the last nine years. But when people meet me, they don't see a depressed, down-on-her-luck person. They see an individual who is enthusiastic about life, enjoys her work, and looks forward to what's next (at least this is what they tell me).

Seeing me, you would not know the situation I am in right now. And do you know why? Because I have learned that circumstances do not define me. I refuse to be a victim! I also have decided to break my life down to basics to learn what really makes me happy. And thus, starting from scratch, once again in 2014, I am in a good place. I can easily say that I am a happy person and life is wonderful.

Has part of my story inspired you a little? I hope so! But let's continue our pursuit of happiness. (I hope no one will be knocking on my door for some royalties.) Let's have a look at a few more simple things that affect all of us on a daily basis. We'll consider food and possessions. And once again, I will bring a few examples from my life.

Although I like to consider myself as a clean eater, I have a downfall – sweets! Just thinking about the baked goodies that my grandmother used to make or a tub of Haagen-Dazs Dulce de Leche ice-cream makes me drool. Those soft, warm pirojki stuffed with ground meat and rice, or the poppy seed roll, or Babushka's famous vatrushki … just one more and I will be so happy! And the sweetness of the caramel taste of Dulce mixed with vanilla ice-cream can make me scream! (Now I've done it. I might have to throw away my car keys so I don't go to the store to buy a tub, and it's on sale!)

I am sure you can think of a few foods in your life that you can have every day because they are tasty and make you feel happy. But do they really? Yes, I get it, they do; in the moment you are enjoying them, you feel content. But what happens after? Well, for me the ice-cream is a sweet trap now. First of all, I discovered that dairy was creating issues for my digestive system and gave it up. Secondly, there is sugar! Should I say more? It is especially unpleasant when you are already a very energetic person by nature. Sugar crashes are bad!

In the past, I could easily enjoy this delicious treat. But now ice-cream does not make me happy! After I have a few spoonfuls, I get bloated, tired, and my face breaks out. And then there are all the calories! Is it worth it? Not for me! Given all of this, it was still not easy to give it up. I am a human being with human desires. In the past, it was a battle to pass the freezer section while my "fave" was on sale and not buy it. I trained myself to remember how many issues I would have after having even just a couple of little spoonfuls of this treat. It worked! And I also found a delicious alternative!

How about possessions? I have a few stories there as well.

I love beautiful and fun clothes. Growing up in Russia, we did not have many choices. Although my parents made sure that I was always dressed well, their budget and the Russian economy did not allow me to have the things that I wanted.

So, when I started making my own money, which coincided with the opening of Russian borders and foreign investments coming in, fun Western fashion was arriving in Moscow. I was very fortunate because I knew English and was young and eager to learn. I held a few high-paying jobs (one of them was at an Italian fashion company) which allowed me to buy sought-after Western brand names.

These were beautiful pieces and cost me a pretty penny. I was in my early twenties, and the future looked bright and prosperous. I continued with my love for beautiful pieces after moving to Canada but realized that things were a little different in this part of the world. Clothing that I wanted for myself or my son was much more expensive and required a lot more of my disposable income.

But I also noticed that I was more obsessive about the care of these material possessions. Every time my little, at the time, son wore a nice piece of clothing, I got upset with him when it got dirty or ripped. I would get angry and get on his case with a lecture of how much this item cost and how hard I had to work for him to have that. Not good! Not a happy feeling! Clothing became more important than my son! A scary concept for me now.

It does not mean my family wears rags now. I still like to dress well and own a nice collection of clothing, but I do not obsess about every new design or trend that comes out. As a matter of fact, trends are not my friends (unless it's a stock market). I have my own style and I am happy with it, and my son learned the same.

As a family, we do not chase possessions. We have a comfortable life with what we have. And if there is something new and shiny that might catch our attention, we have a discussion and consider all the pros and cons before spending our money. We make sure that the purchase has long-term value and hence makes us happy.

So, does any of what you've read so far resonate with you? Do you have your own stories to tell? I am sure you do, and I look forward to hearing them one day. The main idea is to consider things that you think make you happy right now and ask yourself why. If you have a good reason, ask yourself how long something will give you happiness or if it will give you buyer's regret.

With the examples of food and possessions it is easy to understand the idea of temporary triggers of happiness. They wear out pretty fast, and then you have to look for something new or perhaps go to the same temporary triggers just to receive the exact same result.

If we go back to my list, I can explain to you why these things make me happy no matter what is going on around me. Let's take the Sun and Nature. Have you noticed the capitals? Yes, these two are my good friends. And when they are not around, I am a little sad.

The Sun is a source of light for us. It helps to keep the days lit up, it helps to grow food, and it helps us to get a nice suntan on a hot Caribbean beach. I have a special relationship with the Sun. Being an Aries and first zodiac sign, the Sun is my power source. So, I do struggle a little on cloudy days. But this is not the only reason that the Sun makes me happy.

Every day I wake up in the morning, I am super happy and grateful that I have another day to experience the beauty of this powerful star in our sky. I am happy and grateful that it lights up the day even when it's hidden behind the clouds.

On a hot sunny day, I am happy and grateful for its heat and opportunity for things to grow. On a crisp winter day, I am happy and grateful for the bright blue sky and beauty of the snow under the Sun's powerful rays. Have you ever really looked at the snow on a crisp, sunny, winter day? It's magical!

The sun makes me very happy, and I forget about all the troubles I might face that day. Even now I have a big smile on my face despite a heavy winter snowfall outside my window. I remember all of the fun I have had with the Sun.

And, of course, the Sun is the source of life for Nature. Why does Nature make me happy? Well, how about we start with the food we all eat. Where does it come from? Nature. How about most of the houses we live in? Where does the wood come from? Nature. But this is not the reason nature makes me happy.

In the last few years, I discovered that as hard as I tried to run away from Nature, it kept pulling me back in. It's in my blood! I am connected with it. During my spiritual development, I discovered that I was a Natural Healer in several of my past lives. That explained my desire to work in the gardens with plants when I was younger. I had the fortunate circumstance of spending my summers with my grandmother, who had a giant garden full of fruiting trees and shrubs, a variety of berries and vegetables, and countless types of flowers. She worked very hard, and all of us were regular contributors.

Although I enjoyed some of the work, like climbing apple trees and digging for potatoes during harvest season, the watering and weeding parts did not appeal to me. But as I got older, I felt a need to be around plants and get my hands dirty with fertile soil. It felt so good! It made me happy!

Now, I do not have a giant garden yet but I am fortunate to have a few friends who have access to the raw nature, either a home in the country or cottages in the wilderness. At times, I simply escape to the nearby forest for a few hours to meditate. You are alone among trees and birds and never know who might come for a visit: a deer, a fox, a cute bunny.

And then there is foraging (collecting of the wild Nature goodies such as berries, mushrooms, and edible pants)! I can lose myself for hours! I feel completely at home and not at all scared when I am alone in the forest. I talk to plants, trees, and forest creatures and yes, they talk back (that's a whole other book).

Even a winter day can bring pleasure: cross-country skiing and snowshoeing provide great opportunities to see the Nature in its quiet time. But you never know who might surprise you with an appearance. Nature is amazing at any time!

Do you follow me? The idea behind this chapter is to help **YOU** to understand what makes **YOU** happy. There are different states of happiness, and the most basic human needs provide us with short-term happiness. What I would like you to get out of this chapter is to find **YOUR** list of things that make **YOU** happy no matter what – the feeling of happiness that stays with you for a long time. And so, in order to help you, there is your next step – Assignment 2. Have fun, and we'll connect again in Chapter 3.

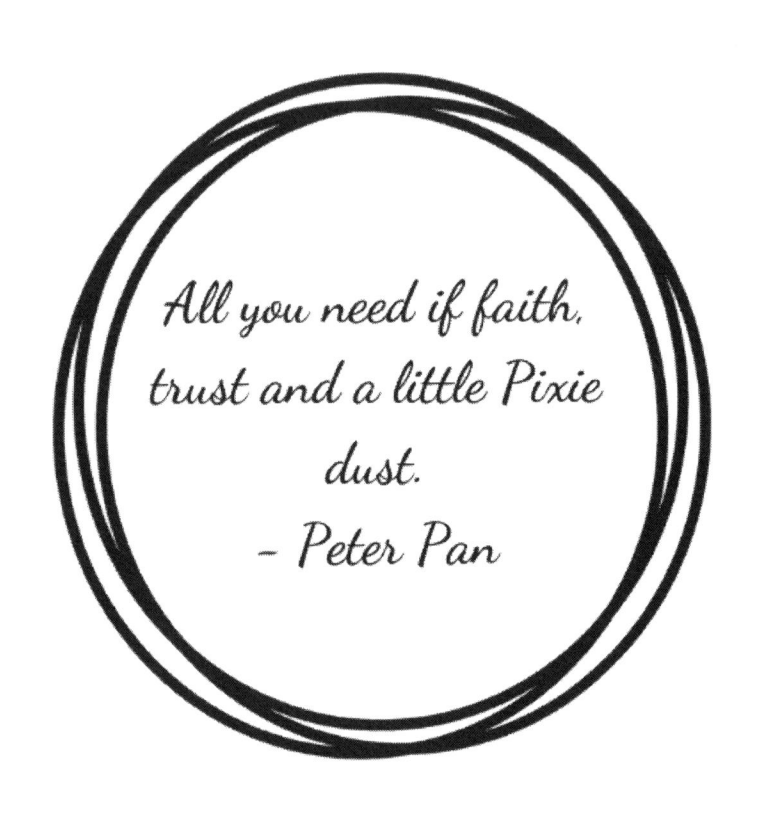

All you need if faith, trust and a little Pixie dust.
- Peter Pan

CHAPTER 3

Things That Interfere with Your Happiness

Now, after a long discussion about the definition of happiness and all the things that make you happy, we are going to look at the "dark side" – we will have a look at things that interfere with your state of elation.

As I am starting to write this chapter, I am sitting in the Warsaw Airport waiting for my flight to Moscow. I am going back to my Motherland to spend time with my family. This should be a happy experience since I have not seen my family in three years. But this trip is rather unexpected and not for a good reason. I am going back to spend time with my Mom and bury my younger brother tomorrow. This is a very sad occasion indeed.

There are many mixed emotions right now. One predominant question is, *could I have done anything to help the situation and make sure that Artiom was still with us?* You see, my brother suffered, suffered for many years, and the last time I spoke with him, he told me that he wanted to die. I burst into tears when I heard him say that since I could not quite understand why someone would not want to live.

And now when his wish was granted by the Universe, I know he is happy and free. He is happy that he does not need to deal with the sadness in his life and struggle through another day. He is happy that he is not in pain anymore. I know that he is happy that our Mom does not have to worry about him anymore. And I know he has freedom from the addiction that brought him this sadness in life and unwillingness to live. He simply could not find happiness in life.

I am still getting used to the idea that next time I go to Russia to visit family, my brother will not be there to greet me, spend time with me, have a conversation with me, and most of all, give me a big hug. It's been a long time since this has happened. The last time I saw Artiom in person was in 2005, and unfortunately it did not end well. I have been back to Russia since, but his lifestyle did not allow us to spend time together. It has not allowed him to be in the same place I was at the same time.

As we remember my brother and move on with our lives, it is incredible how this one moment in life can change everything forever. I am on the plane now, leaving

Moscow behind and heading back home to Canada (yes, this is home now). I cannot stop thinking about my Mom and what will happen next. Yes, it is too early to talk about "now what," but I hope she chooses to be happy.

It is a terrible thing to lose a child and I simply cannot imagine how she feels and, God willing, will never have a chance to find out. All I know is that she was distracted with me being around; and now I am heading back, and she will be faced with the fact that when she goes home, Artiom will not be there. She has been looking after him and caring for him for many years. After saving his life on several occasions and trying to help him to battle through numerous incarcerations, it will be extremely difficult to suddenly not have that need to be helpful.

What I know is that she is a very strong woman, and she will be okay. It will take time, she will grieve, it will be very painful, but she will be just fine, and eventually she will find happiness again. After all she still has my son Daniel and me, her sister, and her cousin's family. Life will have a meaning once again.

I would never have imagined that something like this would be a part of my book, but I believe it is important to discuss death. It is certainly a subject that can make us very unhappy. Some people are not able to recover from the death of a loved one, especially a child. It is a terrible tragedy indeed.

But you must remember that death is a natural occurrence, and we all will die one day. When a young person dies, we say: "She/He died before their time." But how do we know when it is their time? Do you know when it is your time?

Yes, it is very sad since young people usually did not have a chance to experience many things in life as older individuals might have. But this is an erroneous approach in my opinion. If we are to focus on things that might have been, it is the same as focusing on "would haves" and "should haves." These are negative elements of your present and will bring sadness into your life and sabotage your happiness.

Instead, I recommend focusing on the positive: good times you had with this person, memorable accomplishments of this person, and of course this person's smiling face. Celebrate the fact that you had the privilege to know this person. We are all here with a purpose. Even a little baby who may have lived just for one day brought a lot of joy to her/his parents because they had a chance to meet their little angel. Celebrate life! Life is a wonderful thing and the decision of how to handle your reaction to death is in your hands. I promise, you will be happy again.

Now I'd like to move on to more simple matters that can interfere with happiness. Yes, they are not as complex as dealing with death, but they do affect us in a negative way.

We live in the world, which consists of people with different personalities, cultures, and levels of society. (Yes, we will have a look at this as well.) We are all different. I always say: "If we are all the same, the world will be a pretty boring place." I live by these words, and of course, with differences come conflicts, disagreements, and unhappiness.

I can discuss many reasons why living in the world of differences can make us unhappy but there are far too many. What I encourage you to do is to ask yourself why any particular reason makes you unhappy. What's behind it? Is it as simple as your reaction to something that happened? If so, how significant is this event in your life? Will it change your life forever? Could you have reacted in a more positive manner?

A change in your life, an unfriendly face, late transportation, an angry boss – these are just a few examples of infectious unhappiness contributors. I am sure you all experienced one of the above. Perhaps, some may have taken place today. How did you react? Did you blame the person or the event itself? Did this spoil your day? Why? Do you think it was your reaction to the event?

What if you react to the unhappiness contributors in the following way? Embrace the change – change always brings something better. Give a smile to an unfriendly face; acknowledge that sometimes late transportation means a saved life; ask your angry boss if there is something you can do to brighten up her/his day. That's it – just a different way to react to people's actions or the day's events. I understand that this might be easy to do for someone like me, who sees life as a place to have fun and share it with others. But please try to practice a positive reaction to a negative situation. Try it once and you will see the difference. And you will want to try it again and again. The next thing you know, it is just part of your life.

If you are still struggling, we have our "Happiness by You" community to support you. Just visit HAPPINESSBYYOU.COM and help is on its way.

I believe we've paid enough attention to the "dark side." It's time to close the dialogue, analyze what we've learned, and apply it in real life. Are you ready?

Please open your Assignment book and proceed to the page for the Assignment for Chapter 3. No skipping work.

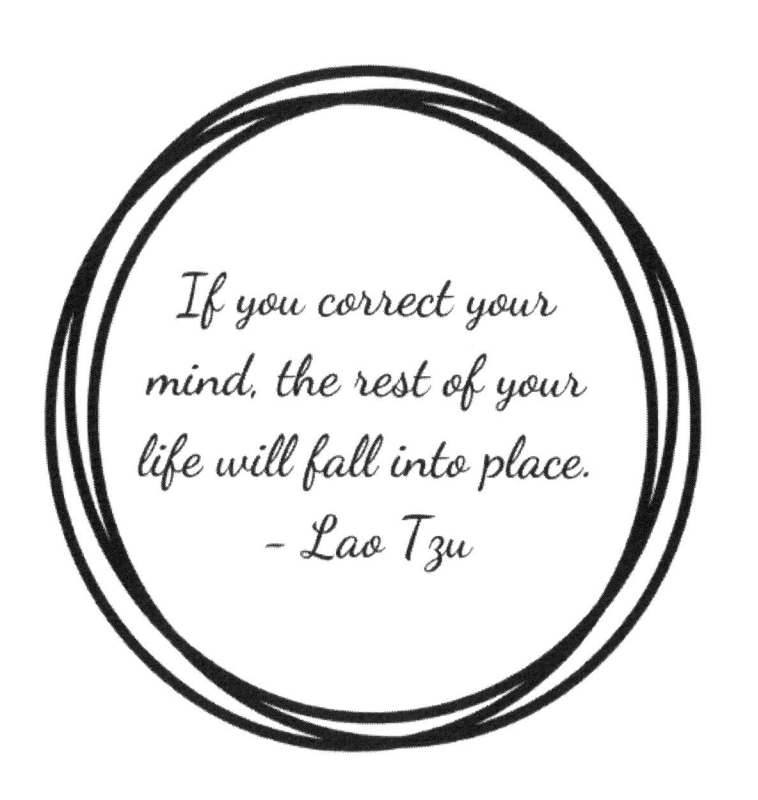

If you correct your mind, the rest of your life will fall into place.
— Lao Tzu

CHAPTER 4

Understanding Yourself

How are you doing? Are you still with me? Ready for more? Well, if you are reading this, I have no doubt that you are with me till the end. Let's continue.

In the previous three chapters, we've learned what happiness is, what makes us happy and how to keep that feeling up for most of the time. Remember, no one is perfect, and that is why life is never boring. Every day challenges present themselves for you to pay attention to. And there is a resolution anxiously waiting to be found and applied. How exciting is that!?

At this point, we've already determined that we are all different: we have different personalities; different sociological and cultural backgrounds; different psychological and physical aspects. And it is suggested by our societies that our life is determined by these.

I will strongly disagree! It is true that these differences have determined part of your personality, but it does not mean that this is who you are. For some people, this idea is quite acceptable, and they are satisfied with living their life as conducted by the society. However, for some it is a continuous struggle to fit the "form" or the "standard" set by someone else to keep order and peace. And yes, I am one of those people who doesn't fit.

My family will hear this for the first time but most likely suspected it for a while. Although I love my family very much and am proud to be Russian, I feel that I never fit there.

Don't get me wrong, I had a great childhood and youth. Both were filled with lots of love from my family. I had many friends; my life was very active with studies; extra-curricular activities, such as sports; political ambitions; and the drive to always be the best at everything. But something was always missing.

Years of life experiences, a move to a different country, and countless hours of self-discovery brought me the answer – although I enjoyed all of the activities, they were all done to prove something to someone, and most likely to fit the "form."

When I look back, it seems that I was always looking for approval from someone. It was either a family member, a teacher or professor, a friend, or a boss. I was once again working hard to prove that I was capable and worthy. And although it seemed that I was progressing, in the end I was not doing anything for me; I was doing it for someone else. I was following the "standard," which was not mine.

So, I discovered the reason for my disappointment in my achievements – what were they for? I started questioning all of that. What was the purpose? What are we here for, to be born, grow up, procreate, and die? That might sound great to most but not to me. The feeling of "there must be something else out there" has been with me since my early twenties. But my search did not start until after a few years in Canada.

As I mentioned previously, I never felt that I fit in when I lived in Russia. And I believe part of it was the ever changing society that was not providing an opportunity for stability. I believe stability is very important for self-discovery. But when you are operating in constant change it is very difficult to focus or plan. I grew up in very uncertain times when it came to basic needs – would banks actually have our money? What was it worth? Would there be food or even clothes in the stores? Would transportation costs be the same as yesterday? No matter how hard you worked to realize your plans, society had other ideas.

A great example is our original departure from Russia for permanent residence in Canada. My husband was

Canadian, and our son was born in Moscow. We were very proud that Daniel had Russian and Canadian citizenship (great hockey genes, yeah!). All documents were ready, tickets were purchased, and a farewell party was planned. We were assured that everything was a go. But at the last possible minute Russian authorities decided that they would not let Daniel leave Russia since he had his own Canadian passport. WHAT?!

It did not make sense, and we were in a state of panic. At the time our son was an 8-month-old. So, after many phone calls and discussions with Russian and Canadian authorities the only solution was to refuse Daniel's Russian citizenship. And yes, this was suggested by Russians. We were upset but there was no other choice at the time. Our perfect plan for dual citizenship for our son was crushed!

Now things have changed in Russia. During my recent visits, it is apparent that people, including my relatives and friends, enjoy a happier and more successful life. However, the ever changing threat is still there, and people are always on alert.

I am very fortunate to live in a great country like Canada, and I remind myself of that every day! Yes, it might not be perfect (there is no such thing as perfection) but it is stable, friendly, open-minded, and healthy. You can make plans and fulfill them. And this is where I started to realize that there is more to life than just going to work, making money, and raising a family. Of course, there is nothing wrong with choosing that way of life; it is one of the foundations for Canadian political and economic stability, but it is not enough for me.

From an early age I wanted to be noticed and, later on, to make a difference in people's lives. I was always looking for that something extra: extra activities, extra questions for homework, an extra few kilometres in my run or cross-country ski; an extra 30 minutes in the gym. It was always a chase to be better and make a difference. And it was nice to have my photo and name on the school boards for academic and athletic achievements; it was fun when my name was brought up to other students after my graduation as an example of a drive to achieve high goals; it was fun to receive trophies and praises. But did it help anyone? Have any of the records set inspired someone to be and do better? I really hope so. But I know that all of these hurt my brother.

With his recent passing at the age of 35, my Mom and I were remembering him in his younger years while I was still living at home. You see, my brother and I have nine years' difference between us, and I do not know much about his life as a teenager or young adult. I was in my last year of high school when he started first grade. Then I moved out of my parents' home when I was 19.

What I know is that he suffered while in school. He was not a great student and always seemed to get in trouble. And it made things worse since most of the teachers rubbed my name and achievements into his face on a daily basis. Who would like that? He was not me! He was an individual looking for his own identity. In his mature years, we spoke about many things, and he told me that I was the person he always looked up to, regardless of the opinions of the teachers and our parents.

Living so far away made it challenging to support my brother. During our phone conversations, I tried to convince him that he was worthy, and I would support him in any way possible. But it didn't work. His life of constant put downs, misunderstandings, and instability led to drug and alcohol abuse, years of incarceration and, ultimately, an untimely demise. He struggled to find his purpose and finally gave up. And it is still very difficult for me to accept that my strong drive, high achievements, and exemplary behaviour could not help one of the closest people to me – my brother.

It comforts my Mom and me that he understood himself: he knew his abilities and his problem areas; he knew his strengths and weaknesses; and closer to the end, he knew that he was losing the battle. But he knew that he was an intelligent and kind person, and he left a lot of heartfelt memories in our minds and warm feelings in our hearts.

But my brother's passing is a great reminder to all of us to live our lives. We all have weak spots that we really struggle with, and it is very important to recognize them, learn more about them, and discover how to manage them. It is great to be a high achiever and an exemplary person but knowing your weaknesses is even more important.

Think about a job interview (I am sure most of you have had more than one). One of the questions usually asked is "What is your weakness?" I remember the first time I was asked that question, I was appalled, embarrassed, and disappointed. How dare they ask me a question like that? I am flawless and that's why they chose me!

Only later in life, I realized that knowing your weaknesses actually helps you. Knowing what might hurt you forces you to be prepared and as a result makes you more effective. And now I also realize that knowing your weak spots makes you a better person. There is nothing wrong with being vulnerable; it makes you more human and people relate to you better.

Another great self-discovery lesson in my life was brought to me by my son. Well, there was more than one, but we will focus on the lesson of perfection or rather "there is no such thing."

For as long as I can remember, I was always a perfectionist. Things just had to be *so*, and it gave me great dissatisfaction if this was not the case, especially if someone else interfered with my perfect "whatever." At that time, it seemed that perfection is what I was: a great student, a great athlete, a perfect child to my parents and grandparents. And all agreed and supported my "perfection." I could do no wrong! And if I did, the first reaction would be: "That could not have been her!" Well, I was not high and mighty, but I always had to prove a point since it was the "right" one.

When my son arrived, of course I was going to be a "perfect" mother and raise another "perfect" human being. If you have children, you are probably laughing uncontrollably right now. What is this word she is using? This does not apply to parenthood! Of course, you might be the "perfect" parent but who am I to judge?

Gone were my perfectly clean and organized apartment, my fun life, my restful nights, and my ability to live life according to me. I adjusted quickly but struggled. Remember, I wanted to be a "perfect" parent. And the ability to be with my son every minute of the day and accomplish everything else was not working so well. Finding a perfect solution seemed impossible.

However, it all became clear to me one day. Daniel was around four years old and really was a "perfect" child. But we were starting to get into "I do not feel like putting away my toys today," territory. That impaired my "perfectly" organized home; this was a threat. And one day I snapped. I got really mad at my little guy and made him cry. This was a turning point in my striving for "perfection."

Suddenly I realized that "being perfect" became more important than my son. What was wrong with me? I became the mother that I tried so hard to avoid. From then on, I understood that there was no such thing as "perfection." Would you agree with me? Even in the "perfect performance" there is always a slight flaw.

I also understood that this was another great opportunity for self-discovery. My "perfect" world collapsed to provide me with opportunities to learn more and become a better parent and human being. Every out-of-the-ordinary event offers a chance to discover a solution and thus challenges you as a person. That in turn leads to self-discovery.

I strongly believe that there are opportunities in life that allow us to be stronger, wiser, kinder, more loving, more grateful, and more vulnerable. Perhaps some of us are so guarded that we do not allow these opportunities to come our way, thus, not allowing further self-discovery. We might be afraid to break our "perfect" stride or worried about societal opinions. I say be more daring, be braver, be curious, be adventurous, and be creative. Let your inner child come out and play! You will be very pleased with the outcome! After all, you will be learning new things about yourself, and knowing yourself will help you to get closer to a happier you.

"What's next?" you ask. Assignment for Chapter 4, of course. No peeking into the next Chapter. See you soon.

Don't be pushed by your problems, be led by your dreams.
- Ralph Waldo Emmerson

CHAPTER 5

Making Choices

Welcome back! Did you have fun with your last exercise? So, what crazy things did you plan for your future?

But don't leave yet; we are not done! This will be a fun chapter. We will be discussing choices. I am sure you had to make quite a few today already. Shall I get up now or stay in bed for another 10 minutes? Shall I have cereal or toast for breakfast? What should I wear today? What shall I have for lunch? And on, and on, and on …

Yes, choices! We all make them on a daily basis. And some you make without any effort; they do not even feel like choices since we make them every day. It's simply a routine. It is an everyday occurrence for every person. We wake up in the morning and decide what needs to be done first. Of course, it depends on what time we woke up. Maybe you do not have time for anything but to get dressed and run. It is still a choice.

Choices are fun. They make us who we are and determine our course in life. I do not believe in wrong choices. I believe the choices that brought unfavorable results help us to learn about our abilities and thus help us with self-discovery. (Remember the last chapter?)

All of us from an early age heard: "This is the wrong thing to do;" "You made a wrong choice;" "I regret my choice." Well, how do the people who make these comments know that? They made choices based on their experience, and the outcome was not favorable.

Now, don't get me wrong, I always listen to people's opinions and some make sense. But I would not jump in a well just because someone else did. It does not sound like fun to me. I will not rob a bank. It feels like a wrong thing to do for me. And I would not drive on the wrong side of the road; I love my life!

I would not follow some suggestions. And not because it is "wrong" advice, but because I foresee a favorable outcome by making an alternative choice.

Time to get into more detail. How do we know how to make choices and expect certain outcomes? Well, it starts from our own experiences and our parents' advice. Remember when your parents told you not to touch the handle of the hot frying pan? What did you do? You touched it anyway. What happened next? You were crying because you burned your hand. Based on that one particular experience, you've discovered that it is not a bad idea to listen to your parents' advice.

And guess what? Here is another good example of choices. You made a choice to not listen to your parents, and the consequence was negative. But based on that you made a choice to listen to your parents from then on (well, probably until your teenage years). So, one experience – two choices.

Of course, this is an oversimplified example. Since then, you have had to face more complex situations that required much more consideration for choices you make. And no matter the choice, there is one thing to follow for sure – consequence. It does not make a difference what the outcome is; the consequence is always next!

The big question to ask yourself is, when presented with making complex choices, are you willing to accept what follows next? It is a very big part of the choice you pick, so you'd better be ready. But there is another option – not to make a choice. And guess what? That is still a choice. Confused?

No problem! Let's have a look at another example. You are not happy with your job and constantly complain about it. Your family and friends are tired of hearing about it and finally one of them (I promise it will be me) suggests that you do something about it.

At first you are shocked at the reaction, as you were probably just looking for sympathy. Then, you get upset and stop talking to that person (me) while still complaining about your job to others. Finally, everyone has had enough and suggests that if you are so unhappy, you really should make a change of some sort. Suddenly you realize that your first friend (me) was right and connect with that person to ask for suggestions on dealing with your situation. Great! You made a first choice – to look at your options. Good luck with step two!

My "smart" parenthetical remarks are not without merit. I love people, but struggle with my affection for the ones who complain about something constantly and do nothing to improve the situation. And their favorite expression is: "I wish …" That's great they have a wish, and I guess you can say that it takes them closer to the solution. But this is not the case. All they do is wish. All I hear is wish I had a better job; wish I made more money; wish I had more time; wish I had her life (this one is very dangerous, but it is another story). You get the idea.

I have complaints as well and, yes, I share them with people. I am an imperfect human being after all. And I have plenty of wishes! But I make a choice to do something about getting closer to the fulfillment of those wishes. Positive or negative consequences, I make choices. And in the process, I learn and am happy to share what

I've learned with people. Just like this book, it has been "coming" for a while and finally made its appearance.

You might think, sure, you have a great life since you are writing a book about happiness. You made all the "right" choices. This could not be further from the truth: I am broke; my personal life is a mess; I had to get a job that pays me well below my worth; I work my two businesses in the evenings and on weekends; I do not have much free time; the only surviving direct member of my family, my Mom, lives in Russia, and I struggle with the guilt of not being there; and my 22-year-old lives with me and is still trying to "discover" himself. But I do not want to complain about any of the above; these have all been my choices. And yes, despite all of that, I am still a happy person!

I mentioned the guilt factor. This is a huge happiness downer. In my life experience, guilt is also a choice. Guilt in my opinion is a negative feeling that is forced on us by society. As I write this part, I have an image of a very serious judge figure slamming the gavel, pointing finger at you and loudly shouting: "GUILTY!"

We feel guilty when we do something wrong. But why do we feel so? Most of the time it is based on other people's opinions. You made a choice and felt it was the right thing to do at the time. But then life events might have thrown you for a loop and all of a sudden you are left with a feeling of guilt.

A personal example of guilt relates to my desire for my Mom to make a choice to come to Canada where she can live with me, her last child, and her only grandchild. She will have a better life (at least that's what I think). But there are plenty of reasons why she would not do this. She is making a choice to stay in Russia. That is the life she knows best and is comfortable with it. I respect her choice. So, I am healing my feelings of guilt by trying to figure out how to help her best from across the ocean.

Choices are crucial for your pursuit of happiness! (Okay, do I pay again?) From learning how to make a decision to considering living with the consequences of your choice – they provide you with opportunities for self-discovery and thus get you closer to the happy state of mind.

Some people have a tough time making choices. My son would be a perfect example. He used to get paralyzed by the decision-making process. "You know I cannot make decisions, Mom," was his excuse when faced with yet another simple, in my opinion, task of making a choice. We worked through that and he is doing much better, although still struggles with more significant life decisions.

And part of his struggle was my overbearing overprotection of him when he was younger. When Daniel was around four, his Dad and I separated. It was my choice and with that came guilt, overprotection, and the creation of my son's dependency on me. Yet, I do not regret any of this since it has been a great learning opportunity for both Daniel and me.

Choices are tricky at times. The one thing that I do not like about making some is that they can hurt other people. However, you are responsible only for your own life, and it is with utmost importance that I encourage you to make choices that bring **YOU** closer to happiness. Yes, it might seem that you hurt other people but, in my opinion, it is their choice to react to your decision in a negative way.

You see, choices you make might not correspond with other people's wishes or expectations. And yes, your choices can make them upset or angry. Their ego is hurt, and ego really does not like that! But if the choice made **YOU** happy, that's all you need to be concerned with. You cannot control how other people react. Remember, it is their responsibility!

That being said, I encourage you to be responsible with your choices. Some might make you happy short term but hurt you in the long run. A good example is related to a healthier lifestyle. Most of us would like to be healthier and have a long, fun, fulfilling, and happy life. So, when you make choices regarding your wellbeing, consider all the consequences.

Are you still trying to convince yourself that it's okay to smoke that one cigarette when you're out with friends? Why? What benefit does it provide you? And how about another sleepless night because you left your big paper that's due tomorrow till the last minute? Are you going to be okay to drive tomorrow? Are we safe in our cars around you?

In conclusion, I would like to remind you that we are the ones responsible for choices we make. And we are responsible for the consequences they bring. When at the crossroads and deciding to stay with the status quo, it is still a choice. Just remember not to complain.

Here is a question: Do you choose to be happy or unhappy? Strange question? Okay. I am sure you will go with the first choice. Here is another question: What do you choose to do to be happy? And here is another one for you: Are you prepared to face the consequences you might face on the way to happiness? Don't worry, the Assignment book is waiting for you to help with finding the "right" answer for you. And for **YOU** only; there are no wrong answers here! To the Assignment for Chapter 5!

There is a huge amount of freedom that comes to you when you take nothing personally.
- kushandwizdom

CHAPTER 6

Happy at Last!

*A*re you happy yet? Great! You're not? Why not? You should be; this is the last chapter. Of course, this is my "funny side" trying to cut in again.

Let's get back to reality and the conclusion of this book. Happiness is a wonderful feeling: it's warm and fuzzy; it brings light and hope; it brings laughter and an overwhelming feeling of satisfaction when you can't stop smiling. We've all been happy at one time or another and when the feeling of happiness comes over us, we know exactly what it is.

Yes, we are at the end of the road with this book, and I would like to make sure that you clearly understand the idea behind it. If at times, even maybe as you are reading this book, you feel upset, disappointed, angry, frustrated, sad, or depressed, it is okay. It is okay to feel any of these feelings. They are simply a part of you, and you would not be complete without them. The important part to remember is that you have a choice. You can choose to feel any of the above and stay that way, or you can feel any of the above and move on. Make a choice not to be stuck with feeling that way for a long time. Having a negative feeling will only attract more of the same, and then it's tough to get out of such a mindset.

I know at times it is easier said than done, and I have been there – stuck in the vicious circle of sadness, dissatisfaction, and negativity. So, I get it; it's not that simple. But I have conquered that obstacle and am here to help you do the same. This is the purpose of this book. Anytime you are struggling to get out of the negative hole, pick up this book and read your favorite part, or go straight to the assignments and practice what I preach (trust me, it works!), or just go to your completed workbook and read through your answers to the assignments. Do whatever it takes to snap out of it by utilizing these tools.

Life is an amazing journey and although sometimes we hear that we have a destiny, it is actually the choices we make that get us there. **YOU** are the driver of **YOUR** destiny. **YOU** are the one who determines what drives **YOUR** life and the events in it. **YOU** are the one who creates magic or a nightmare. **YOU** are the one who chooses to be remembered for all the happy times you had for yourself and shared with others or spent your life complaining and blaming others for your choices. It's in

YOUR hands! So, make a choice to be happy! It will not only help **YOU** but everyone around you.

It is very interesting that, as I am writing the conclusion of this book, I am at the exact same location where I started it. Although this book is not very long, it has taken six months to write. It is a creative process and requires a certain mindset. Of course, many events have taken place during this time. The amazing part is that I mostly remember happy times. It does not mean that there were no sad, frustrating, angry, or disappointing moments. I simply chose not to be stuck there, not to be attached to them for too long. I focused on the positive, the lessons, and the outcomes. I chose the positive way, leading to balance and, eventually, a feeling of happiness.

If you asked me right now what were the most memorable times for me in the last six months, they all would be happy memories, with the exception of my brother's death, of course. Yes, I have reached the point in my life where I can almost shut the negative memories down. It does not mean that I just dismiss them; I deal with them. I pay attention to how I feel, I try to determine why I feel this way, and then I make a choice. And as you can imagine, the choice is pretty simple: stay negative or choose to see the positive. That applies to any negative situation or feeling, no matter what it is. If you are still confused by this concept, I recommend you to go back to Chapter 5, Making Choices, re-read it, and re-do your assignment.

Believe me, it took a few years for me to master this skill of choosing happiness and positive thinking. And since we are all unique, the timing will be different for every one of you. The great part is, if you are struggling, this book should be your first "go-to" tool. If the concept is still a challenge, I will be happy to help you to decipher your puzzle of happiness during a group or one-on-one session. And, of course, there is our monthly newsletter and "*happy*" community. Just head to **HAPPINESSBYYOU.COM** and join the party. Remember, you are never alone!

As my final word, I would like you to know how grateful I am for your support! Thank you for choosing to spend your time to give this book and me a chance. Thank you for believing that happiness is achievable, and **YOU** are the one who can navigate **YOUR** life into a more positive direction. **YOU** are the master of **YOUR** destiny and all **YOU** have to do is to start learning about yourself and how to make choices that enrich **YOUR** life and eventually the lives of people around you. So, stay happy and help others to do the same! The world can certainly use more happy people.

You are almost there. There is just one more request and one more Assignment. Please google Bob Marley's "Three Little Birds," listen to the song, and pay attention to the lyrics. Life is only as complicated as we make it! So, take it easy and be happy!

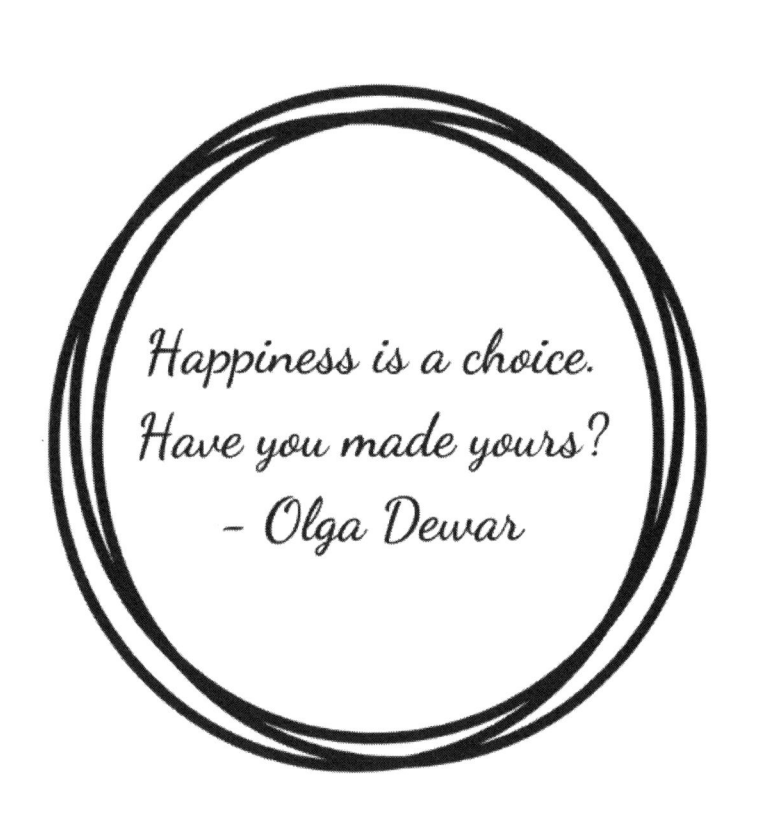

*Happiness is a choice.
Have you made yours?
— Olga Dewar*

About the Author

Olga Dewar calls Ottawa, Canada, her home. She is originally from Moscow, Russia, and has been calling Canada her home since 1995.

Olga is one of the happiest people in the world, yes, almost all of the time.

She is a lover of life and a lover of nature and everything alive. She is a forager. If you cannot find her, she is most likely in the forest looking for mushrooms, berries, or getting lost in the beauty of His Majesty the Forest and hugs of Mother Nature. She is a fitness and healthy lifestyle enthusiast. She is a practitioner of chemical-free living and a spiritual being – OMMMMMMM.

Yes, she is all of the above and more. She loves new beginnings, creating, and executing. She loves helping, learning, educating, and sharing.

Her favorite colour is blue – like gorgeous blue sky and waters of a sea or an ocean. Her favorite flower is a Sunflower – it reminds her of a gorgeous sun in the blue sky.

She loves little kids and their innocence. They remind her that all of our minds were pure and unencumbered by the nonsense of societal standards when we were little. That allowed us to be us and see the world for what it really is.

How do you like her so far? Well, she hopes you actually like her. "I know, presumptuous," she would say.

She is an Aries and yes, everything the horoscope says about them is true, although over the years, she has learned how to manage the negative traits and turned them into positive outcomes.

She loves people, even the grumpy ones – we all have bad days.

Two of her strongest traits are patience and understanding. The first one made it to her wrist as a tattoo on January 2018. It is a constant reminder of how important patience is in her life – especially as an Aries. Yeah, they want whatever they want yesterday.

She struggled, she stumbled, she failed, she lost. She was scared, she was unsure, she was frightened, she was devastated, she was broken, she was broke, she was overwhelmed, and she had to start over many times. But she survived, she's accomplished, she succeeded, she overturned, she rose, she leads, and she lives!

Over the years, Olga learned that happiness is our responsibility and only we can make ourselves happy. Our actions, our reactions, our decisions, and our solutions are the way to more happiness every day. She loves her life and, yes, she is a Joy Aficionada!

Questions? Seriously, if you have any, and Olga is sure you do, just reach out. She is here to support you and help you to get where you'd like to be on your happiness scale.

Thank you for purchasing and reading the **"Happiness By You"** book. I hope you enjoyed it and learned a few things.

This is a starting point for anyone who wants to bring more happy hours, days, weeks, and years to their life. This is a textbook that you can return to over, and over, and over again. Of course, the workbook is another great companion that can help you to practice what you learned.

If you want to continue developing and learning even more, now there is another option available to you. **"Discover Your True Happiness"** is a self-study course that is now available to you on-line. Here is what you'll discover in this course:

- **Learn of more ways for self-discovery and understanding**
- **Learn more about your true happy triggers**
- **Learn how to utilize your happy triggers more often**
- **Learn more about your unhappy triggers**
- **Learn how to eliminate and manage your unhappy triggers**
- **Learn how to make decisions with more confidence**
- **Learn how to appreciate the choices you make**

If you are committed to making your life the best it can be, enroll in this course and join our **Happiness By You private group**. This group offers additional resources, live events, and surprises.

www.happinessbyyou.com/course
For questions, reach out to **olga@happinessbyyou.com**.
See you inside **HBY Community**!

Sockathon

We need them all! No matter how big or small.

Sockathon is an initiative that was started by me in 2014. It came about as an idea to support a few less fortunate families in my community by providing them with warm socks to help with cold winters in Ottawa. This amazing initiative now has grown to not only provide warm socks to the less fortunate but support a few other charitable initiatives that help single moms, women and children that escape abusive relationships, and many more shelters in the Ottawa area.

To support more people, I created an on-line donation option and also negotiated with a few local retailers. This allows me to purchase in bulk and stretch every dollar.

Donations are now coming from all over the world and you can help as well. Every dollar counts!

Please visit www.happinessbyyou.com/sockathon

Did you know that socks are the most requested but least donated item in shelters in North America? Your support is invaluable. Let's grow this initiative across North America.

For any questions you can reach me at olga@happinessbyyou.com.

HEARTS to be HEARD

Giving a Voice to Creativity!

With every donation, a voice will be given to the creativity that lies within the hearts of our children living with diverse challenges.

By making this difference, children that may not have been given the opportunity to have their Heart Heard will have the freedom to create beautiful works of art and musical creations.

Donate by visiting
HeartstobeHeard.com

We thank you.

Manufactured by Amazon.ca
Bolton, ON